LEWIS ALEXANDER

Decorations by
AARON DOUGLAS

DREAMSONGS
& other
P O E M S

FORGOTTEN POETS

Editor | Dick Whyte   Number 14 | 2023

❧

LEWIS G. ALEXANDER (1898-1945) was born in Washington D.C. and attended Howard University, and later the University of Pennsylvania, both known for their support of African American students. Alexander started writing poetry at the age of 19, and was one of the earliest non-Japanese poets to specialise in English-language tanka and hokku, drawing on the work of John Gould Fletcher and Yone Noguchi, alongside translators like W.G. Aston and Basil Hall Chamberlain. Alexander would go on to publish tanka, hokku, and both rhymed and 'free' verse, in numerous well-known arts and poetry magazines throughout the 1920s, including *The Crisis*, *Opportunity*, *The Messenger*, and *Fire!!*. Alexander was also a playwright, director, actor, and costume designer. At university he joined the Howard Players, and then the Washington Play-Writers Circle, directing the Randall Community Center Players and the Ira Aldridge Players of the Grover Cleveland School. During the 1922-1923 seasons Alexander joined the Ethiopian Art Theatre group, appearing in productions of Oscar Wilde's *Salome*, and William Shakespeare's *The Comedy of Errors*.

❧

Publication credits: 'Hokku I–XIV' (*The Crisis*, Dec. 1923), 'XV–XXXIII' (*Opportunity: Journal of Negro Life*, Sep. 1925), 'XXXIV–XLIII' & 'Tanka I–VIII' (*Caroling Dusk*, ed. Countee Cullen, 1927), 'XLIV–XLIX' (*Black Opals*, Dec. 1927); 'Africa' (*Opportunity*, May 1924); Enchantment I & II' (*The New Negro: An Interpretation*, 1925); 'Streets' & 'Little Cinderella' (*Fire!!*, Nov. 1926); 'Negro Woman' (*Opportunity*, April 1926); 'Transformation' (June 1927); 'Day & Night' (Dec. 1927); 'The Dark Brother' (*Caroling Dusk*, 1927); 'Effigy: Form & Fashion' (*Ebony & Topaz*, 1927); 'Dream Song' (*Palms*, Oct. 1926); 'Tobacco Factory Girl' (*The Messenger*, Feb. 1927); 'Durham Streets' (June 1927); 'A Tree' (*The Crisis*, May 1928); 'Quest' (July 1928); 'Barefoot Blues' & 'Tree Meditation' (*Carolina Magazine*, May 1928); 'Memory' (Nov. 1928); 'Nocturne Varial', 'My Body', 'Wishes', 'Sympathy', 'Atonement', & 'My Epitaph' (April 1929); 'An Essay: Japanese Hokku' (*The Crisis*, Dec. 1923), etc.

Cover: Silhouettes from *Fire!!* (Nov. 1926) & *Carolina Magazine* (1928). Inside; Aaron Douglas – 'Three Line Drawings' (*Fire!!*, Nov. 1926); & 'Three Silhouettes' from *Opportunity* (Feb. & June 1926) & *Carolina Magazine* (1928) & various ornaments from *Caroling Dusk* (1927); 'Roses' (*The Crisis*, Oct. 1924), etc.

FORGOTTEN PRESS
Aotearoa | New Zealand

ISBN: 978-1-991310-06-4 (paperback) ● 978-1-991310-07-1 (hardback)
978-1-0670081-7-8 (ebook)

Lewis G. Alexander
Dream Songs & Other Poems

Hokku & Tanka

Lewis Alexander's complete hokku and tanka,
first published 1923-1927.

Poems

A selection of verses, rhymed & unrhymed,
first published 1924-1929.

Essays

Two short essays: *Japanese Hokku* (1923)
& *Georgia Douglas Johnson* (1928).

FORGOTTEN POETS

edited by **Dick Whyte** .

Missing Meters! Lost Lyrics!
Vanished Verses!

LEWIS ALEXANDER
PEARL ANDELSON
IRIS BARRY
GWENDOLYN BENNETT
ADELAIDE CRAPSEY
MARY CAROLYN DAVIES
HILDA DOOLITTLE
HILDEGARDE FLANNER
F.S. FLINT
JUN FUJITA
SADAKICHI HARTMANN
T.E. HULME
TAKEKO KUJO
AMY LOWELL
MINA LOY
YONE NOGUCHI
CHARLES REZNIKOFF
EDWARD STORER
MARIE TUDOR-GARLAND
AKIKO YOSHINO
AKIKO YANAGIWARA
& MANY MORE

FORGOTTENPOETS.COM

HOKKU & TANKA

Like cherry blossoms
Dancing with the passing wind—
My shattered hopes.

Night shadows woo me:
I cling to the crescent moon
    Like the evening star.

When the last leaf falls
Summer will be thought of more,
Winter having come.

My soul like a tree
Sways above dry-leaf Autumn:
Be kind, oh wind-god.

Last night I saw you,
A dream rose and I your stem;
Showing you the sun.

You walk before me,
I will follow where you go;
Though I be wary.

White dogwood blossoms
Cling to the curving branches
Like I cling to you.

The drooping willows
Have the charm of waterfalls
Above the river.

They tear at my heart—
The days that knew no desire—
For they were wasted.

No words speak louder
Than the tragic look of eyes;
Close yours out your love!

A wood violet
Alone in the spacious hut
Worshipping the sun.

The bird is alone
Like a dot on a blue page:
Do not set red sun.

O apple blossoms
Give me your words of silence!
Yes, your charming speech.

Life is history
Turn not away from the book:
Write on every page!

Life goes by moving,
Up and down a chain of moods
Wanting what's nothing.

My soul is the wind
Dashing down fields of Autumn:
O, too swift to sing.

Knowing not at all
Who stands above me seeing:
Tears of gratitude.

The nightingale sings
My heart desires but the night
Space swallows my voice:

Listen to the rain
Falling broken on the ground:
Pity the sky once.

Did you say a sound?
Did you say the wind? Dashing?
Only my soul's quick—

O moon of tonight
Let me rest my head on you
And hear my life sing.

I shall spend my moods
Like a rose discards leaves
And die without moods.

My ears burn for speech,
And you lie cold and silent.
Supinely cruel:

Look at the white moon
The sphinx does not question more.
Turn away your eyes.

Thought that is no thought
Poems buried in my heart
Song that is no song . . .

Treading wearily
A unit of the parade
There is no escape.

I ride down the stream
Between the earth and the sun
On the moon's shadow.

The poetry of life?
No, the picture of my dreams
Flashing on my heart.

My heart like a shell
Moans at the breast of the earth
Being too full to sing.

You are life's fountain
Springing from eternity
Flow not recklessly.

Within the shadow
I am weaving the pattern
Of a spider web.

Sitting by the pool,
I looked in and saw my face.
O that I were blind!

Why should I wander
I who have known no surprise!
Every day the same.

I will wrap the song
In the leaves of the lotus
And send it to you.

If you would know me,
Do not regard this display;
Mingle with my speech.

Why sit like the sphinx,
Watching the caravan pass?
Join in the parade.

What if the wind blows?
What if the leaves are scattered,
Now that they are dead?

While trimming the plants
I saw some flowers drooping—
I am a flower.

This is but my robe,
His Majesty gave to me.
Garments will decay.

On the flowering twig,
Lo! The robin is singing.
It must be spring.

Looking up the hill
The road was long before me.
This road is longer.

Death is not cruel
From what I have seen of life;
Nothing else remains.

If you had not sung
Then what would I imitate,
Happy nightingale?

I am but a leaf
Clinging to the tree of life
In the world's garden.

The moon—ah the moon
Draped in the velvet of night
Brocaded with stars.

Do not bring lanterns
I say, "Darkness is supreme
Delight beyond words."

Drops of silver blood
Are falling from the sky's heart.
All the world has woe.

O night of shadows
Seal my lips with your magic
Of silent beauty!

The wind is a comb
Fixing clouds about the moon
In a strange coiffure.

So this is the reed?
The very pipes for singing—
Life plays me new songs.
Wistfully from out the dawn
The crows broke across the sky!

Drink in moods of joy!
Why should the sky be lonely?
Neither sun nor moon—
How my heart is shy of night
Like Autumn's leaf brown pendants.

Cold against the sky
The blue jays cried at dawning.
The larks where are they?
Heavily upon the air
My ears tuned in to listen.

Could I but retrace
The winding stairs fate built me.
They fell from my feet.
Now I stand on the high round.
Down beneath height above depth—

Through the eyes of life
I looked in at my own heart:
A long furrowed field
Grown cement waiting for seed
Baking in desolation.

Could I hear your voice
O but this silence is sweet
Words mar all beauty.
Turn then into your own heart
And pluck the roots from the soil—

By the pool of life
Willows are drooping tonight
I can see no stars.
What dances in the water?
O my clouds dripping with tears.

And now Spring has come
Blossoming up my garden.
I alone unchanged.
Moving in my house of Autumn.
One leaf alone saves a tree.

POEMS

Streets

Avenues of dreams
Boulevards of pain
Moving black streams
Shimmering like rain.

Negro Woman

The sky hangs heavy tonight
Like the hair of a Negro woman.
The scars of the moon are curved
Like the wrinkles on the brow
    of a Negro woman.

The stars twinkle tonight
Like the glaze in a Negro woman's eyes,
Drinking the tears set flowing
    by an aging hurt
Gnawing at her heart.

The earth trembles tonight
Like the quiver of a Negro woman's eye-lids
    cupping tears.

A f r i c a

Thou art not dead,
      although the spoiler's hand
Lies heavy as death upon thee; though the wrath
Of its accursed might is in thy path
And has usurped thy children of their land;
Though yet the scourges of a monstrous band
Roam on your ruined fields, your trampled lanes,
Your ravaged homes and desolated fanes;
Thou art not dead, but sleeping,—Motherland.

A mighty country, valorous and free,
Thou shalt outlive this terror and this pain;
Shall call thy scattered children back to thee,
Strong with the memory of their brothers slain;
And rise from out thy channel house to be
Thine own immortal, brilliant self again!

Little Cinderella

Look me over, kid!
    I knows I'm neat,—
    Little Cinderella from head to feet.
    Drinks all night at Club Alabam,—
    What comes next I don't give a damn!

    Daddy, daddy,
    You sho' looks keen!
    I likes men that are long and lean.
    Broad Street ain't got no brighter lights
    Than your eyes at pitch midnight.

Enchantment

I. NIGHT

The moonlight:
Juice flowing from an over-ripe pomegranate
bursting

The cossack-crested palm trees:
motionless

The leopard spotted shade
inciting fear

silence seeds sown . . .

II. MEDICINE DANCE

A body smiling with black beauty
Leaping into the air
Around a grotesque hyena-faced monster:
The Sorcerer—
A black body—dancing with beauty
Clothed in African moonlight,
Smiling more beauty into its body.
The hyena-faced monster yelps!

Echo!
Silence—
The dance
Leaps—
Twirls—
The twirling body comes to a fall
At the feet of the monster.
Yelps—
Wild—
Terror-filled—
Echo—

The hyena-faced monster jumps
starts,
runs,
chases his own yelps back to the wilderness.
The black body clothed in moonlight
Raises up its head,
Holding a face dancing with delight.

Terror reigns like a new crowned king.

Transformation

I return the bitterness
　　Which you gave to me,
When I wanted loveliness
　　Tantalant and free.

I return the bitterness;
It is washed by tears;
Now it is a loveliness
Garnished through the years.

I return it loveliness,
Having made it so;
For I wore the bitterness
From it long ago.

The Dark Brother

"Lo, I am black but I am comely too,
Black as the night, black as the deep dark caves.
I am the scion of a race of slaves
Who helped to build a nation strong that you
And I may stand within the world's full view,
Fearless and firm as dreadnoughts on rough waves;
Holding a banner high whose floating braves
The opposition of the tried untrue.

Casting an eye of love upon my face,
Seeing a newer light within my eyes,
A rarer beauty in your brother race
Will merge upon your visioning fullwise.
Though I am black my heart through love is pure,
And you through love my blackness shall endure!"

D a y & N i g h t

The day is a Negro
  Yelling out of breath.
The night is a Negro
  Laughing up to death.

The day is a jazz band
  Blasting loud and wild.
The night is a jazz band
  Moaning Blues songs, child.

The day is the sunshine
  Undressed in the street.
The night is the sunshine
  Dressed from head to feet.

I am like a rainbow
  Arched across the way.
Yes, I am a rainbow
  Being night or day.

Effigy

FORM

You stood in the yard
Like a lilac bush
With your head tossed high
As if to push
Your hair in a blossom
About your head
You wore the grace
Of a fragile reed.

FASHION

Your gown cackled loud
Like the swish of leaves
Being flitted about
By a lyric breeze
Your step was like a dainty fawn
Breathing the nectared air at dawn,
Oft have I seen the rose in you
But it never bloomed such a brilliant hue.

Dream Song

Walk with the sun,
Dance at high noon;
And dream when night falls black;
But when the stars
Vie with the moon,
Then call the lost dream back.

The Tobacco Factory Girl

I wonder
If the man
To whom she gives her love:
Sees her as the mother of his children,
Or the woman for his body's pleasure?

The sad black girl upon his arm
Goes to the factory each morning at seven.
She works beside him the hours through.
They trudge down Pettigrew Street each dusk.
She is his daily companion, his choice.
She is snubbed by the shoppers
    of Fayetteville Street;
Who forget that she makes them.
I wonder if her husband too forgets?

    I wonder
If the man
To whom she gives her love:
Sees her as the mother of his children,
Or the woman for his body's pleasure?

Durham Streets

Feet
F-e-e-t

Faces
F-a-c-e-s

Bodies
B-o-d-i-e-s
Tobacco scented B-O-D-I-E-S

The Durham streets at dusk
Are swarmed with color.

It is the moving panorama
Painted by the factory artist
Each dusk.

A Tree
[*To M. V. C.*]

(Leaves)

Tender green eyes flashing,
To catch the eye of God
Thanking him for bounties
Flowing from the sod.

(Branches)

Praying arms outstretched
To the silent sky,
Penetrating vastness
For a mute reply.

(Body)

A brown gnarled vase
Lacquered with bark.
The resting place
Of a singing lark.

(Roots)

Tiny tripping toes
Pivoted in soil
That the swaying body
Never may recoil.

(L'envoi)

The dance of leaves is a beautiful thing.
The lyric of branches sweet.
The cry of a body bent by the wind
And roots rumbling in retreat.

Tree Meditation

How very like a tree
Alas am I
And like to bursting blossoms
Are my thoughts.
Some will remain upon the tree
And fruit
And others fall
And drift far on the stream.

For those that drift
There shall be no returning;
But those which fruit
Shall burst and scatter seed.
The seed shall stand
A flowering tree again
Each generation stronger than the last.

I'm but the tree!
Would I were soil or water
I could not face the agony of death—
Eternally to mother tree and seedling
And breathe the beauty of the blossom time.

Being the tree
I needs must face the shedding
Bear the fruit which bursts
And flowers which fall;
Standing helpless see them drift down stream
    To sea—
Where there shall be no coming back!

Q u e s t

Like roses ramble on the ground
   And up the trellised porch,
I have sought you all around
   Baring brave the torch.

Now the lengthy search has burned
   Out the flaming light.
I with broken heart return
   Searching thru the night.

Nocturne Varial

I came as a shadow,
  I stand now a light;
The depth of my darkness
  Transfigures your night.

My soul is a nocturne
  Each note is a star;
The light will not blind you
  So look where you are.

The radiance is soothing.
  There's warmth in the light.
I came as a shadow,
  To dazzle your night!

Memory

Forget? God grant I may forget.
　　But ah, the tortured I;
While winding down the trail, regret
　　I can't but breathe a sigh.

You ask too much to say, forget!
　　When you have rent my heart;
And bleeding sores are open yet
　　From your rude arrow's dart.

My Body

My body is an instrument,
  Play it you who will;
But they who touch the vital chords
  Music will distil.

Let's say it is a violin,
  Or better still a reed;
Through which to play a tune, Marlyn,
  To sate your every need.

Wishes

O, for a breast to weep upon
   The tears that fain would flow,
For I am weighted down with grief
   No other heart could know.

O, for a dark abyss in which
   I soon could lay my head;
And slumber on and dream and dream
   'Til earth gives up her dead.

And waking find that which was grief
   Consumed by time's decay,
Feeling my spirit wing the heights
   Against the light of day.

S y m p a t h y

I have dreams of my own,
  You need not dream for me;
Far better I alone
  Than in your company.

Though sympathy may lead
  You to my door ajar,
Leave me still, to read
  Dreams in a little star.

B a r e f o o t B l u e s

It was dead winter time
Ma feet flat on de groun'.
It was dead winter time
And ma feet was flat on de groun'
A've been all ovah town
And no work can be foun'.

Went to de lunch room
To try to git a bite to eat,
Ah went to de lunch room
To try to git a bite to eat,
Because ah had no money
De man he put me in de street.

'Cause ah had no room rent
De lady had ma stuff fo' sale,
'Cause ah had no room rent
De lady had ma stuff fo' sale,
And when ah tried to git it
De man he put me in de jail.

Now ah'm blue, weary and blue,
Barefooted and in de jail.
Ah mean blue, oh so blue,
Barefooted and in de jail.
Ah'll shut mah mouf an' stay here
'Cause ain' nobody goin' mah bail.

Atonement

That day was gray—
So gray, so gray,
And not a rain drop fell
To fill the vacancy left by
The broken hearted bell.

And I alone—
Alone, alone!
Wept 'til my eyes wold high,
And oh how I wept in silence;
Heaving not a sigh!

My Epitaph

I am no better than the birds that sing,
So when I die do not bring me flowers.
Dig no grave, erect no monument;
But lay me high upon a lonely hill
As close as possible to God's window sill
    called heaven.

Let birds of prey come feed upon my body,
And when my bones of flesh are empty quite
Let them remain 'til time has played its part.
The sun and wind and rain and time alas—
Shall dwindle them to nothing but white dust.
Then let this dust commingle with the hill,
And drift downward into some hungry stream;
There to be lost forever to men's sight.
    I need no grave.
        I need no monument.

ESSAYS

JAPANESE HOKKU

The Crisis (1923)

According to John Gould Fletcher, one of the foremost modern students of Japanese Literature, "really authentic information on Japanese poetry does not date further back than the 6th century, AD. But at this point the germ of its later development can easily be perceived. The poems of this early date were composed of a first line of 5 syllables, and a second of 7, and so on always ending with a line of 7 syllables followed by one of equal number. Thus the entire poem of whatever length (a poem of 40 lines was scarce, even at that day), always was composed of an odd number of lines, alternating in length of syllables from 5-7 until the close, which was an extra seven syllable line. There were no other rules. Rhyme, accent, quantity, stress, were disregarded.

Later this crystallized into what is called a Tanka or 'short ode'. This was five lines in length constructed syllabically 5, 7, 5, 7, 7, or thirty-one syllables in all. Innumerable of these Tanka were written. Gradually during the Feudal period, improvising verse became a pastime in court circles. Some one would utter the first three lines of a Tanka and some one else would cap the composition by adding the last two. This division persisted. The first hemistich which was composed of 17 syllables grew to be called the Hokku. The second or finishing hemistich of 14 syllables was called the Ageku. Thus was born the form which is more peculiarly Japanese than any other.

Composing Hokku might however have remained a mere game of elaborate literary conceits and double meanings, but for the genius of one man. This was the great Bashō (1644-1694) who may be called the greatest 'epigrammatist' of any time. During a life of extreme and voluntary self-denial and wondering, Bashō obtained over a thousand disciples and to found a school of Hokku writing which has persisted down to the present day. He reformed the Hokku by introducing into everything he wrote a deep spiritual significance underlying the words. He even went so far as to disregard upon occasions the syllabic rule and to add extraneous syllables, if thereby he might perfect his statement. The most famous Hokku that Bashō wrote might be literally translated thus:

An old pond
And the sound of a frog leaping
Into the water.

This means nothing to the western mind. But to the Japanese it means all the beauty of such a life of retirement and contemplation as Bashō practised. If we permit our minds to supply the detail which Bashō deliberately omitted, we see the mouldering temple enclosure, the sage himself in meditation, the ancient bit of water, and the sound of the frog's leap—passing vanity—slipping into the silence of eternity. The poem has three meanings: 1) First it is a statement of fact; 2) Second it is an emotion deduced from that; 3) Third it is a sort of spiritual allegory. All this Bashō has given us in his seventeen syllables."

To paraphrase Yone Noguchi: "To say that a Hokku is a seventeen syllable poem with five syllables in the first line, seven in the second and five in the last is not enough. There is more, naturally, than its mere form. Its real value is not in its physical directness but in its psychological indirectness. To use a simile it is like a rain drop with the sun shining on it as it falls; although it is just a bit of water it shines, glitters, and sparkles now red, then purple, turquoise-blue, opalescent, and pearl-white.

The real value of the Hokku is not in what is said but what is suggested. The object of the Hokku poet is to impress the reader with the high atmosphere in which they are living." The emotions they express are too subtle for words and can only be written in the spaces between the lines as in conversations there are thoughts which the conversants can never convey as they cannot be clothed in speech, being too subtle for words. Here out of the love which I have for these delicate little petals that carry a rose in their fragrance, I beg to offer some of my Hokku poems;

Like cherry blossoms
Dancing with the passing wind—
My shattered hopes.

A wood violet
Alone in the spacious hut
Worshipping the sun.

You walk before me,
I will follow where you go;
Though I be wary.

The bird is alone
Like a dot on a blue page:
Do not set red sun.

A WOMAN'S LOVE LIFE

Carolina Magazine (1928)

With the appearance of Georgia Douglas Johnson's *Autumn Love Cycle*, we have but another reason for acclaiming her the foremost woman poet of the Negro Literary Renaissance. The heart of womanhood speaks as in her first book, but with more intensity, finer feeling, greater felicity and surer abandon. Her message is stripped bare of superfluities; thereby making it more human and stronger in appeal because of its utter simplicity.

Begin the cycle with the poet, "I closed my shutters tight last night" and as it were you are concealed in a sanctum with an exceptional soul who pours its heart throbs out to you like pearls from a time lashed river bed. Her pen does not stride nor does it flash; but moves quiescently despite the turbulent agencies which are the impetus.

The emotions expressed stir the heart, heat the brow; but the poet holds herself in sweet control. Hardly can one find lovelier lyrics than 'Proving', 'A Paradox', 'Welt', and 'Review'.

The cycle is divided quite ingenuously into five sections, one lacing naturally into the other. Many a sonnet sequence has been written, but this is the most consistently arranged lyrical sequence that has come beneath my notice. The thing itself is a distinct contribution to the poetry of the world, for without a doubt it is universal in appeal and for that reason deserves a very wide reading. *An Autumn Love Cycle* contains some of the most beautiful lyrics of this age, and Love, the world old theme, is very refreshingly used. To get a better understanding of the eternal feminine read *An Autumn Love Cycle*. That you may get a retrospective view of a woman's love life, read this pageant in rhyme. After reviewing all its tragic charm, I was indeed greatly relieved by the lines from the beautiful summarizing lyric 'Afterglow';

> *For every glancing golden gleam,*
> *I offer gladly—pain*
> *And I would give a thousand worlds*
> *To live it all again.*

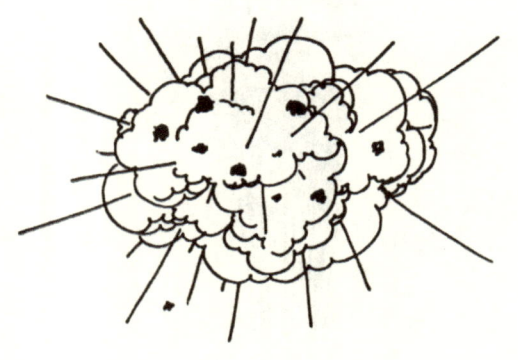

This Space for Your
Thoughts

THE OLD EXPRESSIONS ARE WITH US ALWAYS
AND THERE ARE ALWAYS OTHERS

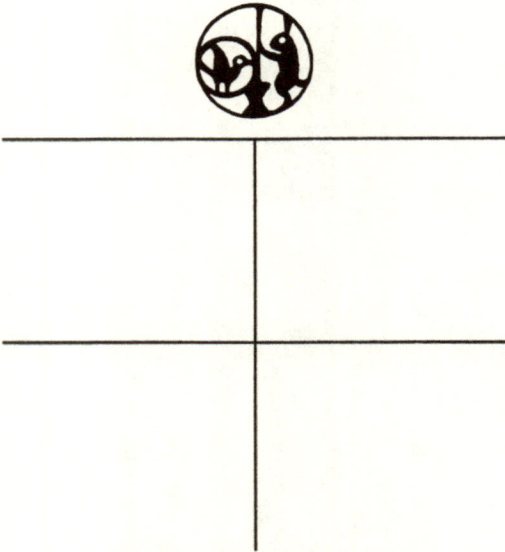

Please handle with care.